River of Life

PIONEER EDITION

By Karen Ross and Elizabeth Sengel

CONTENTS

River of Life

BY KAREN ROSS

Thirsty animals gather at this river in Africa. They have come to the right place.

Meeting Place. *Large and small animals come together to drink from the Okavango River.*

What is the most valuable thing in the world? It depends on where you live. In Botswana, a country in Africa, the answer is water. Little rain falls, so the Okavango River is very valuable. It brings much needed water.

This river begins far away. After flowing many miles, it spreads out into different streams, forming a **delta**. People and animals come to the delta to find water and food.

Water World

The river is a good way to travel. I am riding in a canoe with guides, who belong to a local group of people. They push our boat through the water with a wooden pole.

We glide past beautiful water plants. Small birds fly by quickly, and tiny frogs hide in flowers. I hear a cry above and look up.

It is a big African fish eagle. The bird rises up and swoops down. It plucks a fish from the water to eat.

Termite Islands

We see tiny islands dotted with fruit trees. From the boat, I see berries and figs. We stop for a break in the shade, and I snack on the sweet, brown fruit of a palm tree.

I think about how the islands formed. Insects called termites made giant **mounds**, or hills, when the land was dry. When the river flooded, the hilltops stayed above water. They became islands. Seeds landed there, and trees grew to cover the islands.

Water World. *The river is important to the people who live near it. The river gives people what they need to survive.*

Above the Okavango Delta

Hundreds of islands dot the Okavango Delta. The maps show the delta during the wet season and the dry season. How does the area change?

Rain and floods spread water. This makes the wetlands grow larger.

In the heat, water dries up. That causes the wetlands to shrink.

Life on the River

I finish my fruit and I hop back into the boat. As we continue south, the guides talk to me. Their speech sounds like music.

They tell me about village life. The people get almost everything they need from the river. Women make baskets from palm leaves. Nearly everyone fishes. Men use nets, while women place long baskets underwater. Children chase fish into the baskets. Babies watch the action. They sit in little baskets that are strapped on the backs of their mothers.

Watching Animals

As we float past the last islands, we see larger animals. I spot zebras eating grass, while buffalo cool off in the water. Everything seems peaceful. Yet I know it is not.

Big cats come here. These lions, leopards, and cheetahs are hungry. The smaller animals fear them. So they walk and watch quietly.

I spot African wild dogs. Few are left in the wild. Working in packs, they kill large animals. Then they eat fast. After all, big cats like free meals, and they might steal the dogs' food.

Looking for Lions

I hear a lion roar. A pride of lions is in the water. The adults are wading. The cubs swim, bobbing their heads up and down. They look cute, and I laugh as I watch them.

Yet I wonder, too. Most cats hate to get wet, so these lions must be hungry. They are crossing the river to find food. The cats hunt many animals along the river. They also look for animals that others have killed.

What's for dinner? *This lion hopes to catch a buffalo for supper. Lions hunt and eat other animals.*

Gone Fishing. *These women will use their long baskets to catch fish.*

King of the River

People say lions are the kings of the jungle, but elephants rule this delta. I see elephants of all sizes. As the younger ones play, the adults watch out for the babies. To scare away lions, they stamp their feet.

Botswana has about 100,000 elephants, more than any other country. They are the largest land animals. They are also the second tallest. Only giraffes are taller.

Elephants at Work

Elephants are strong. They carry hundreds of pounds with their trunks, and they use their heads to push things over. An elephant knocks down a tree so that it can munch the tender top leaves. Elephants eat grass, water plants, and fruit trees.

Elephants do important work in nature. During dry months, parts of the river dry up. Elephants find underground streams. They dig holes and drink their fill. Then other animals drink what is left. This **system** works out well for everyone.

Danger at the Delta

Life at the delta is hard. Sometimes there is too much water, and at other times there is not enough!

Getting water is not easy. It is dangerous for smaller or weaker animals to search for water. Bigger animals hunt them.

All the same, animals come to the delta. The delta means water, and water means life.

delta: fan-shaped area at the mouth of a river

mound: a large round pile of dirt

system: way of doing something that follows a plan

Big Boss. *Forget lions. Elephants are really in charge at the delta.*

Water Fun. *Hippos pass the day by playing in water.*

A Day in the Delta

By Elizabeth Sengel

Elephants

Adult elephants and their babies drink water from the river.

Hippopotamus and Fish Eagle

A fish eagle sits on the back of a hippopotamus. Hippos spend their days resting in the water.

The fish eagle flies over the river to catch a meal!

Crocodile

A fierce crocodile climbs out of the water. People in the delta fear these large reptiles.

Lions

A young lioness looks into the camera. It follows other lions as they cross the river.

Cheetah

At the end of the day, a cheetah stands on top of a termite mound. The mound is useful. It provides a good lookout point for surveying the land.

Delta Days

Take a trip down the river and answer these questions about the Okavango Delta.

1. How do islands form in the Okavango Delta?
2. The Okavango Delta helps people survive. What things do people get from the delta that help them?
3. Why do elephants rule the Okavango Delta?
4. How do different kinds of animals use the Okavango River?
5. Why is the Okavango a river of life?